W9-CDV-718

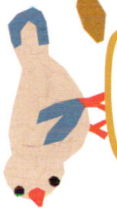

One Million Trees

A True Story

Kristen Balouch

Margaret Ferguson Books
Holiday House · New York

*I loved my math class and knew I would miss it.

What I packed.

We left our
little red house
in California and
flew to Canada, where
we switched to a seaplane.
Then we flew over mountains,
between mountains, and
around mountains,
before landing on the water
next to a little town
on Vancouver Island.

We motored to a dock where a crew of 24 Canadians who mostly spoke French met us with trailers, campers, and trucks.

Rosemary

Claude

Simon

Pierre

Aimée

Dr. Cello

Byron

Martha

Elvie

Vince

Gee

*Bonjour, mes amis (pronounced bawn-zhoor mays ah-mee) = Hello, my friends

Inside the trucks were boxes, and inside the boxes were . . .

Baby trees raised in trays are called plugs by horticulturists, people who are expert gardeners.

TREES!

One MILLION of them!

Each truck had 500 boxes of trees.

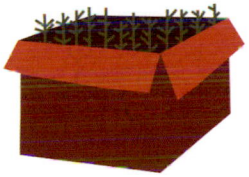

Each box had 500 baby trees.

How many trees were in 1 truck?
*500 x 500 = ?**

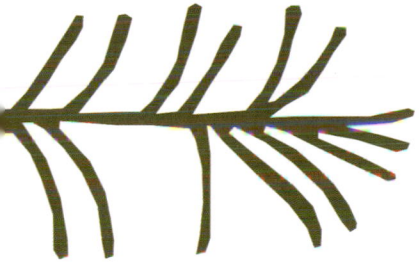

How many trucks did it take to hold 1 million trees?
*1,000,000 ÷ number of trees in a truck = ?***

*250,000 trees in each truck ** 1,000,000 ÷ 250,000 = 4 trucks

We drove along a narrow, curvy, bumpy road until we came to a river, where we set up camp.

Our tent

Cook shack

*Fish = poisson (pronounced pwa-sawn)

The crew even brought a bathtub.

Dad set up our tent.

*Tree = arbre (pronounced are-bruh)

The cook shack was a truck outfitted with a stove, refrigerator, and sink!

The cooking pots were so big that my sister Erin could hide in them.

Mom organized the cook shack. She was going to be the camp cook.

*Merci (pronounced mehr-see) = Thank you

The next morning everyone ate breakfast,
then grabbed their lunches and tools.
My sisters and Wonder Dog stayed with Mom,
but I went with Dad. I wanted to help him plant trees.

Dad drove one of the trucks to the planting site.

The road hadn't been used for a long time.

There were some obstacles.

Mothership was our home-base bus at the planting site.

*Bear = ours (pronounced oors)

*Moose = élan (pronunced ae-lawn) *Whale = baleine (pronunced bah-len) *Elk = wapiti (pronounced wa-pee-tee)

When we finally made it to the site, there were tree stumps everywhere.

It felt empty and lifeless.

Dad, what happened here?
Loggers cut down all of the trees.
WHY?
To use the wood to make things like houses, light poles, and toothpicks. The trees we plant will replace the cut trees.
But how will we ever plant a million of them?
You'll see.
Wow! We use so much wood.

Box of trees

Dad and I got our first box of trees from the truck and he showed me how to plant them.

1. DIG

Depending on the species, choose a spot to plant the tree:

on a mound (water drains away and the soil stays drier)

in a depression (water collects and keeps the soil moist)

near a stump (protects a baby tree from harsh weather)

in a rotted tree (feeds a baby tree with rich organic material)

under a bush (protects a baby tree from harsh sun)

We planted trees in rows, and once we got to the end of a row, we turned around and planted a new line of trees back toward the truck. Each person (my dad and I counted as one person) planted two boxes a day.

2. WEDGE
Make a V-shaped opening in the soil with a shovel.

3. TUCK
Tuck the tree in along the back side of the shovel.

4. PAT
Use the toe or side of your boot to fill in the dirt around the tree.

Once we were done, checkers came by and tugged on the trees.

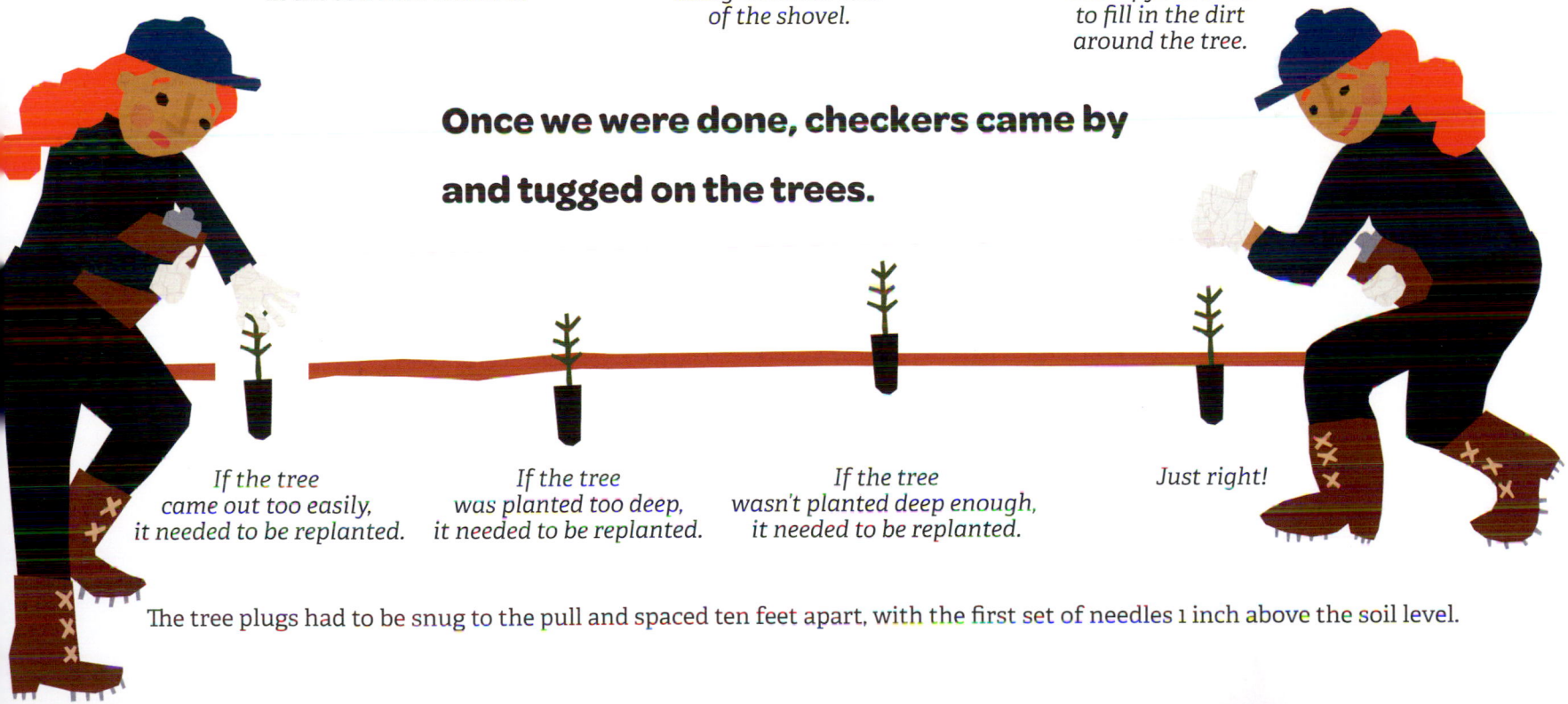

If the tree came out too easily, it needed to be replanted.

If the tree was planted too deep, it needed to be replanted.

If the tree wasn't planted deep enough, it needed to be replanted.

Just right!

The tree plugs had to be snug to the pull and spaced ten feet apart, with the first set of needles 1 inch above the soil level.

Most days I helped Dad. But some days I did my schoolwork and explored or swam with my sisters and Wonder Dog.

Old trees sometimes fall on the ground in the woods and baby trees grow out of them.

Mom says
the number of tree rings
tells how old the tree is.
450 rings mean this
tree is 450 years old.
Wider rings mean conditions
were good and nutrients were
plentiful for the tree that year.
*Turtle
*Turtle = tortue (pronounced tor-too)

And some days I helped Mom by making dessert for the crew.

Planting trees made everyone hungry, and Mom had to make a lot of food.

Some Desserts I Made

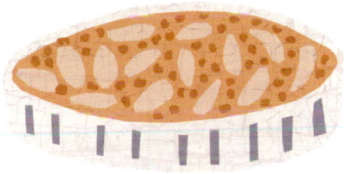

I made 4 apple crumbles.
Each crumble needed 6 apples.

How many apples did I use?
*6 + 6 + 6 + 6 = ? or 4 x 6 = ?**

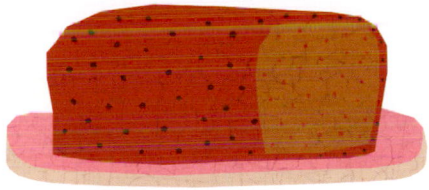

I made 3 loaves of banana bread.
Each loaf needed 4 bananas.

How many bananas did I use?
*4 + 4 + 4 = ? or 3 x 4 = ?**

I made 2 chocolate cakes.
Each cake used 4 eggs.

How many eggs did I use?
*4 + 4 = ? or 2 x 4 =?**

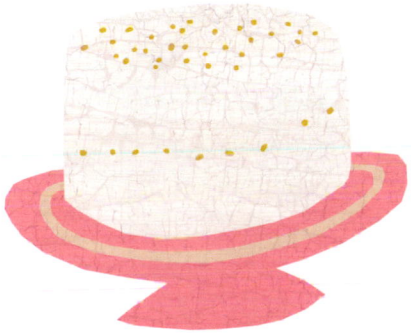

I made 2 lemon cakes.
Each cake needed 6 lemons.

How many lemons did I use?
*6 + 6 = ? or 2 x 6 = ?**

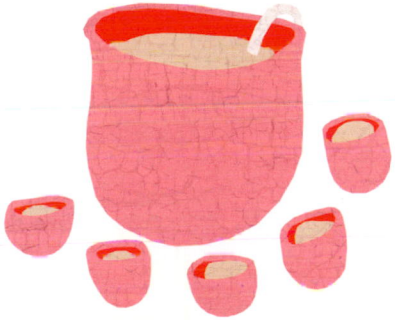

I made 4 batches of rice pudding.
Each batch needed 1 cup of rice.

How many cups of rice did I use?
*1 + 1 + 1 + 1 = ? or 1 x 4 = ?**

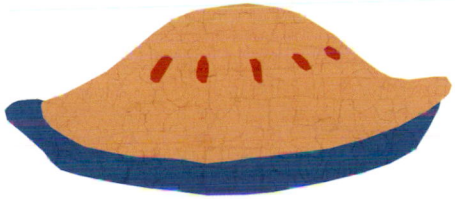

I made 4 rhubarb pies.
Each pie needed 8 stalks of rhubarb.

How many stalks did I use?
*8 + 8 + 8 + 8 = ? or 4 x 8 = ?**

*Apples = 24 *Bananas = 12 *Eggs = 8 *Lemons = 12 *Cups of rice = 4 *Stalks of rhubarb = 32

*C'est bon (pronounced say bawn) = It's good *Fox = renard (pronounced ruh-nar)

After 40 days of planting, the tree boxes were empty. The food was gone. Everyone was covered in mud, scratches, and bug bites. But we all went to sleep happy because...

We did it! We planted one million trees!

*Fini (pronounced fee-nee) = Finished *Youpi (pronounced you-pee) = Yay *Hourra (pronounced hoo-rah) = Yippee

We said goodbye to the trees,

swam one more time in the river, and broke down camp.

*Au revoir (pronounced oh ruh-vwar) = Goodbye

Forty years passed.

And today when my children return home from college,

I hand them suitcases. There is something I want us to see.